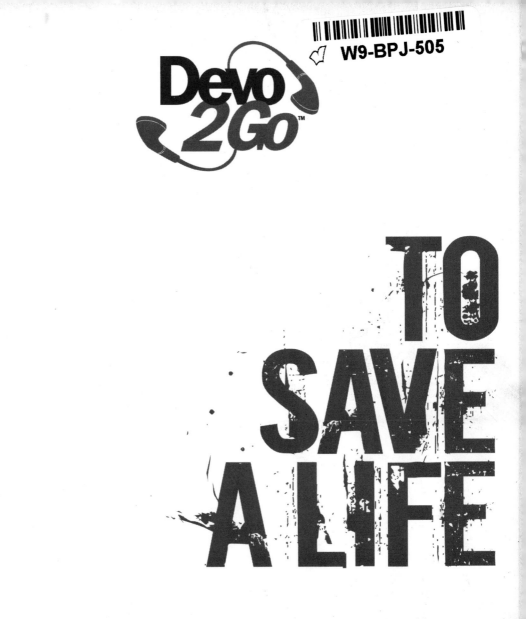

OUTREACH®

Outreach, Inc., Vista, CA
Outreach.com

Graphic Design and Layout:
Christen Bourgeois

Editing:
Jennifer Dion
Toni Ridgaway

ISBN 978-0-9823744-5-0

4. DO THE DEVOTIONAL EVERY DAY >>
In each daily session, you will listen to a few minutes of teaching. When the teaching is done, pause the audio and take a few moments to focus and get rid of distractions. Pray and ask God to speak to you. Then, with the help of your guide, complete the day's devotion by answering the questions and writing your thoughts in your *Devo2Go*™ journal. Play the audio to hear your guide review each question, then pause the audio while you record your thoughts.

5. GET SOME ACCOUNTABILITY >>
The Christian life was never meant to be lived alone. We need to push and encourage each other in order to grow. Get some friends to do the *Devo2Go*™ with you, so you can kick it around together afterwards. They can get a copy of *Devo2Go*™ at a local bookstore. Your friends can even try the first week of *Devo2Go*™ *free*! They can download the *free* version at **Devo2Go.com**. Encourage your friends to check it out!

6. GIVE YOURSELF LOTS OF GRACE >>
If you miss a day, don't stress over it. Simply start up the next day and catch up later, or just finish later.

Meet your *Devo2Go*™ narrator, Josh Weigel.
Visit him online @ **ToSaveALifeMovie.com**.

SHOW LOVE

HEY— ONE LAST THING...

EXPECT GOD TO SHOW UP! Before Jesus got a hold of His twelve disciples, they had all walked through town hundreds of times on their way to work. It was not until they walked with Jesus that they began to notice the hurting, the lonely, the lost, and the left-out. It's also when they started to notice the miracles flowing from Jesus like water from a fire hydrant. Get ready to be blown away!

HAVE YOU EVER BEEN TO A MUSEUM WITH A SELF-GUIDED TOUR?

You put on headphones and listen to a tour guide describe the exhibits and point out stuff you would have otherwise missed. In a lot of ways, *Devo2Go*™ works like a tour guide through the Bible, and each week you will have a different guide to walk you through your devotionals.

Below are some steps that will help you get the most out of *Devo2Go*™— and ultimately encourage you as you grow in a relationship with God.

1. DOWNLOAD DEVO2GO™ TO YOUR COMPUTER & MP3 PLAYER >>
Devo2Go™ comes with a graphic, interactive player. You can play *Devo2Go*™ on your computer, MP3 player, or an MP3-compatible CD player or phone. Follow the download instructions on the *Devo2Go*™ player to download the audio files.

2. DOWNLOAD THE INTERACTIVE JOURNAL >>
See the instructions on the inside back cover of your journal for information on how to download the interactive version of this journal.

3. COME PREPARED TO READ THE BIBLE AND RECORD YOUR THOUGHTS >>
You can use an actual Bible and your *Devo2Go*™ printed journal, or if you prefer to do *Devo2Go*™ online, you can use the interactive version of the journal with Web links to Bible sites and other cool info.

It's important that you don't just listen to your guides, but you also really interact with the Bible verses and study questions. While your guides are very knowledgeable, you will learn the most when you discover the truth yourself instead of just hearing it. The guides will also help you interact with Scripture, but ultimately you are the one taking the journey.

HOW TO USE

Devo 2Go™

Contents

MEET YOUR GUIDES

Josh Weigel NARRATOR

(Josh Weigel photo within LISTEN UP! graphic)

LISTEN UP!

Josh has been in the film industry for over ten years. He started acting in commercials and short films before landing the role of the youth pastor, Chris Vaughn, in *To Save A Life*. These days, Josh writes and produces movies that focus on faith and social justice. He lives in the Los Angeles area with his wife, Rebekah, and their three children.

Visit Josh online @
ToSaveALifeMovie.com.

Jim Britts : WEEK 1

Jim is the author of *To Save A Life*. He is passionate about working with teens, and for the last ten years has been the pastor of the Souled Out youth ministry at New Song Community Church. (You can see Jim's church, home beach, and cool black Jeep in the movie!) Jim has a degree in film and hangs out in Southern California with his wife, Rachel.

Visit Jim and check out *To Save A Life* stuff at **JimBritts.com**.

Zach Hunter : STUDENT PERSPECTIVE *for all weeks*

Zach is a teenage author, speaker, and activist who spends much of his time talking about God's heart for the poor and oppressed. When he was twelve, he founded Loose Change to Loosen Chains, a student-led campaign to end modern-day slavery. Zach has written three books and speaks to hundreds of thousands of people each year, inspiring them to find their passion and make a change in the world. Zach lives in Atlanta with his parents and brother.

Learn more about Zach and his ministry at **ZachHunter.me**.

Brooklyn Lindsey : WEEK 2

Brooklyn, a former model and beauty queen, is the author of two books, including *Confessions of a Not-So-Supermodel*. She is also a youth pastor at a church in Florida and loves hanging with teens, teaching from the Bible, and leading people to live in response to God's love. She lives in Florida with her husband, Coy, and their daughter Kerri.

Get the latest on Brooklyn at **BrooklynLindsey.BlogSpot.com**.

Megan Hutchinson : WEEK 3

Megan is a veteran youth leader who works with hurting teens worldwide. She co-wrote *Life Hurts—God Heals*, an eight-step recovery program for teens struggling with emotional pain and/or addiction; she's also co-written several other books for hurting teens. Megan and her husband, Adam, can be found at the beach making sandcastles or surfing with their two boys, Jack and Parker.

Learn more about Megan at **LifeHurtsGodHeals.com**.

David Hasz : WEEK 5

David works with Teen Mania Ministries in Texas, challenging teens to take Jesus' life-giving message to the ends of the earth. He directs Teen Mania's Honor Academy, an intensive program designed to power a passionate pursuit of Jesus. David's wife, Beth, is a cancer survivor; they have four children and live in East Texas.

Check out David and Teen Mania at **TeenMania.com**.

Leeland+*Jack* Mooring : WEEK 4

Leeland and Jack are the front guys for Leeland, a GRAMMY®–nominated rock band. Their newest album, *Opposite Way*, calls this generation to live passionately for the Lord, even when it means going the "opposite way" of the world. Leeland became a Christian at age five and wrote his first song at eleven. He describes himself as "hyper, driven, and fun." Jack plays keyboard for the band and calls himself "nice, fun, serious, and semi-dorky."

Visit Leeland and enjoy their music at **LeelandOnline.com**.

Miles McPherson : WEEK 6

Miles is a guy radically transformed by God. A former defensive back for the San Diego Chargers, he overcame a crippling drug habit to form Miles Ahead, an organization with a mission to reach one million teens with the Gospel. He serves as senior pastor for The Rock Church in downtown San Diego and has written five books. Miles and his wife have three children and live in California.

Hang out with Miles at **MilesMcPherson.com**.

WEEK '1

Lowering the Waterline

[DEVOTION]
DAY 1

The two most important questions you need to ask in life are, "Is there a God?" and if so, "What does He want with me?"

Maybe you would say, like Jake, that, "My life is fine." But God wants your life to be *WAY MORE THAN FINE.*

Relax ┊ PRESS ⏸

Take a moment to identify the distractions around you and in your mind, and set those aside. Ask God to speak to you as you go through today's devotional.

Read ┊ LUKE 9:18–27

"But what about you?" he asked, "Who do YOU say I am?"

—*Jesus to His disciples*

Relate ┊ STEP INTO THIS PASSAGE OF SCRIPTURE

For a few moments, really try to get an understanding of the teaching and how it applies to your life.

1. Why do you think Jesus asked the disciples who the crowds thought He was? Jesus was God; He obviously knew His identity, so why ask?

2. Why do you think Jesus asked the disciples specifically who they thought He was? What was Jesus' reaction when Peter gave the right answer?

PRESS PAUSE ⏸ BETWEEN QUESTIONS
to reflect and write your answers.

Check It Out: If you are unsure about who Jesus was, visit Devo2Go.com and click on **what's God all about**.

3. Jesus made a clear distinction between what the crowds believed about Him and what His disciples believed about Him. Why do you think Jesus distinguished between the two groups?

ReACT

4. Imagine you are sitting there with the other disciples and Jesus asks you the question, "Who do you think I am?" What would you say?

VERSES 23-27 describe the life to which Jesus was calling His disciples. Jesus knew the disciples could not live out that life (of denying themselves and taking up their crosses) if they did not fully understand who He was. The same is true today; we need to know Jesus as God in order to love other people and put their needs above our own.

HEY— ONE LAST THING...

Even completing this *Devo2Go*™ series will take devotion, but you can do this! Faith is a journey, and the journey is not so much about a destination as a transformation.

SHOW LOVE

YOUR PRAYERS + THOUGHTS

You're on **DAY 1** of your journey. Check off each day as you complete it.

Week 1	**1**	2	3	4	5	6	**7**
Week 2	**8**	9	10	11	12	13	**14**
Week 3	**15**	16	17	18	19	20	**21**
Week 4	**22**	23	24	25	26	27	**28**
Week 5	**29**	30	31	32	33	34	**35**
Week 6	**36**	37	38	39	40	41	**42**

WELCOME TO THE JOURNEY!

(VULNERABLE)

DAY 2

HAVE YOU EVER FELT VULNERABLE?
Do you ever think about being vulnerable before God? Today, we're going to look at a powerful passage written by a guy named David who absolutely knew what it was like to feel vulnerable.

PRESS PAUSE ⏸ **BETWEEN QUESTIONS** to reflect and write your answers.

Relax · PRESS ⏸

Take a moment to identify the distractions around you and in your mind, and set those aside. Ask God to speak to you as you go through today's devotional.

Read · PSALM 139: 1–14

"You have searched me, Lord, and you know me."
—*King David*

Relate · STEP INTO THIS PASSAGE OF SCRIPTURE

For a few moments, really try to get an understanding of the teaching and how it applies to your life.

1. How did David, the author, feel about being vulnerable before God? Why do you think that was?

2. David is describing his own relationship with God, but the lesson applies to all of us. How are you also vulnerable before God?

3. According to this passage, where does God like to spend His time and with whom?

4. How passionate is God about the details of your life?

NOTE: *This passage is not God describing David as "fearfully and wonderfully made," but it is David himself discovering how God sees him and how God made him. He's overwhelmed by God's love for him.*

ReACT

David's response to being vulnerable before God is found in verses 13-14.

5. Take a minute to write your own response to God about the fact that He created you and fully loves you.

HEY–
ONE LAST THING...

God chooses and has always chosen to see the best in you. If you're going to live in a way that helps others experience love, it's gotta start with the truth that God truly loves you.

SHOW LOVE

YOUR PRAYERS + THOUGHTS

Week 1	1	2	3	4	5	6	7
Week 2	8	9	10	11	12	13	14
Week 3	15	16	17	18	19	20	21
Week 4	22	23	24	25	26	27	28
Week 5	29	30	31	32	33	34	35
Week 6	36	37	38	39	40	41	42

GOD LOVES You!

(CHOSEN)

DAY 3

Most people see the Bible as a list of *DOs* and *DON'Ts*, but when you really open the book up, it reads a lot more like a love letter from God to us.

Today, as you open the Bible, read it like a love letter from God to you.

PRESS PAUSE ⏸ BETWEEN QUESTIONS
to reflect and write your answers.

(18)

Relax : PRESS ⏸

Take a moment to identify the distractions around you and in your mind, and set those aside. Ask God to speak to you as you go through today's devotional.

Read : EPHESIANS 1:3–14

"For he chose us in him before the creation of the world to be holy and blameless in his sight."

—*The Apostle Paul, writing to the Ephesians*

Relax : STEP INTO THIS PASSAGE OF SCRIPTURE

For a few moments, really try to get an understanding of the teaching and how it applies to your life.

1. Write down everything Jesus has to say about you according to this passage. *(For example, verse 3 says you are blessed.)*

2. Look at the list you just wrote. Imagine God sitting across the table saying each of these things to you. How do you think you would respond?

3. Before reading this passage, how did you believe God viewed you? In what ways does this scripture affect your view of yourself?

ReACT

Jim told a story about how an upcoming wedding changed his view of the "big picture."

4. How can seeing the "big picture" from God's perspective change your day-to-day life?

5. Go back to the list you wrote for the first *Relate* question. Choose one statement from the list and write a few sentences thanking God for seeing you this way.

HEY—
ONE LAST THING...

What if you trained yourself to focus on how God sees you every time you started to get frustrated or discouraged with life? What if you realized that God sees everyone else in the same way?

YOUR PRAYERS + THOUGHTS

Week 1	1	2	**3**	4	5	6	7
Week 2	8	9	10	11	12	13	14
Week 3	15	16	17	18	19	20	21
Week 4	22	23	24	25	26	27	28
Week 5	29	30	31	32	33	34	35
Week 6	36	37	38	39	40	41	42

DAY 4

Have you ever wondered, "Is there really a point to life?"

God does have a purpose for life, including yours. He has *BIG PLANS* for you!

PRESS PAUSE  **BETWEEN QUESTIONS** to reflect and write your answers.

[20]

Relax   PRESS

Take a moment to identify the distractions around you and in your mind, and set those aside. Ask God to speak to you as you go through today's devotional.

Read   EPHESIANS 2:1–10

"For we are God's handiwork, created in Christ Jesus to do good works, which God prepared in advance for us to do."

—*The Apostle Paul, writing to the Ephesians*

Relate   STEP INTO THIS PASSAGE OF SCRIPTURE

For a few moments, really try to get an understanding of the teaching and how it applies to your life.

1. According to verses 1-3, what were you like before you accepted Christ in your life? Write down some of the words the Bible uses to describe your old self.

2. According to verse 4, what happened? How does Jesus change us and our lives?

3. According to verses 8-9, how were we saved? Have you accepted that gift?

ReACT

You're not saved by your actions or works, but you were saved for action. Not just any run-of-the-mill action, but a mission specifically for you, that God had in mind before He even created you. One day we're going to bow down before this loving God and He's going to ask, "So what did you do with that mission I gave you?"

4. If you have no idea what God has in store for you, that's OK, but spend some time today writing a prayer to God asking for direction. If you have an idea what God might be calling you to, write it below and then pray for God to give you strength to truly live it out.

HEY— ONE LAST THING...

SHOW LOVE

In the very same verse where you were referred to as God's masterpiece, you are also told that God has a specific mission for your life. When you live out the mission God created you to do, it's then that He whispers in response, "My masterpiece!"

YOUR PRAYERS + THOUGHTS

Week 1	1	2	3	**4**	5	6	7
Week 2	8	9	10	11	12	13	14
Week 3	15	16	17	18	19	20	21
Week 4	22	23	24	25	26	27	28
Week 5	29	30	31	32	33	34	35
Week 6	36	37	38	39	40	41	42

Check It Out: If you haven't accepted God's gift, check out Devo2Go.com and click on **accept God's gift**.

WHAT'S YOUR MISSION?

[REPUTATION] DAY 5

The word *HYPOCRITE* comes from the Greek, meaning "someone who is acting." If we're going to live like Jake in the film and save lives, we must start with examining ourselves and asking whether we are truly living out our faith.

PRESS PAUSE ❚❚ BETWEEN QUESTIONS to reflect and write your answers.

Relax : PRESS ❚❚

Take a moment to identify the distractions around you and in your mind, and set those aside. Ask God to speak to you as you go through today's devotional.

Read : REVELATION 3:1–3

"I know your deeds; you have a reputation of being alive, but you are dead. Wake up!"

—*The Apostle John, to the church in Sardis*

Relate : STEP INTO THIS PASSAGE OF SCRIPTURE

For a few moments, really try to get an understanding of the teaching and how it applies to your life.

1. Imagine you are a part of the Sardis church. What is your reputation, according to this passage?

2. How do we sometimes still do this very thing in today's world?

ReACT

If Jim, your **Devo2Go**™ *guide, got a chance to hang out with some people from school who know you pretty well, and he said,"Tell me about _____," what would they say about you?*

3. Below, write some of the words you think they would use to describe you.

Now imagine Jim got a chance to hang out with God for a little while, and he asked God, who knows everything, "Tell me about _____."

4. What would God say?

5. Compare the two answers. Are there areas in which you have a reputation for doing good but really, you're "faking it"? List any ways in which your faith is more an act than truth.

6. Before moving forward in this guide, is there any area you need to confess to God and ask for strength to live differently? *(Use the space below.)*

HEY— ## ONE LAST THING...

Tell someone who you really trust what you've committed to God so they can keep you accountable. Most of the commitments we make without telling anybody end up being the commitments we don't keep.

SHOW LOVE

YOUR PRAYERS + THOUGHTS

Week 1	1	2	3	4	**5**	6	7
Week 2	8	9	10	11	12	13	14
Week 3	15	16	17	18	19	20	21
Week 4	22	23	24	25	26	27	28
Week 5	29	30	31	32	33	34	35
Week 6	36	37	38	39	40	41	42

Visit Jim and check out *To Save A Life* stuff @ **JimBritts.com**.

BE ALIVE FOR GOD!

[23]

DAY 6

This week, one of the most profoundly simple ideas is that God loves YOU. Maybe you've heard this idea before, but it hasn't really taken root in how you view yourself and how you view God.

For Tomorrow...

ON DAY SEVEN, take the opportunity to go to church, attend your youth group, or pray and review this week's devotions.

PRESS PAUSE ⏸ **BETWEEN QUESTIONS** to reflect and write your answers.

Relax : PRESS ⏸

Take a minute to quiet yourself and ask God what He wants to teach you today.

Read : PSALM 25:4–10

"According to your love remember me, for you, Lord, are good."

—*King David*

Relate : STEP INTO THIS PASSAGE OF SCRIPTURE

For a few moments, really try to get an understanding of the teaching and how it applies to your life.

1. Maybe you've had some tough teachers—teachers you thought were really demanding or unfair, teachers who wouldn't give you a break. What do you think God would be like as a teacher?

In the film **To Save A Life**, Jake tells Amy that she's spent her whole life trying to get others to love her.

2. Are there ways that you try to earn peoples' love and acceptance, or even God's? How does this contrast with the Psalmist's picture of God as a teacher and lover of people?

Check It Out: Maybe you have a friend who needs to know today that God loves them. **Invite them to do this devotional with you!**

3. According to verse 7 of Psalm 25, what's the difference between God looking at you through your sins and rebellion versus God looking at you through the lens of His love?

ReACT

If you've been holding on to past mistakes and haven't accepted God's forgiveness for them, take care of that now.

4. Ask God to forgive you so you can start fresh. Take a moment to write this as a prayer to God.

Maybe you've already taken your offenses and sins to God and asked him to take away the weight of the guilt and shame. If you're still feeling accused and unloved, you should know these feelings are not from God. He loves you in spite of your sin or selfishness, and if you've asked for forgiveness in a specific area then you need to let the guilt go.

5. What do you think God is trying to tell you about how he sees you in spite of your sin and shortcomings?

HEY— ONE LAST THING...

SHOW LOVE

As Jim said, God sees you as His incredible creation. His love for you is greater than anything you could have done—greater than your weaknesses that seem to stare you in the face. He is crazy about you and wants to use you to show His love to others. So *shame off you*—go live in His love today!

YOUR PRAYERS + THOUGHTS

Week 1	1	2	3	4	5	**6**	7
Week 2	8	9	10	11	12	13	14
Week 3	15	16	17	18	19	20	21
Week 4	22	23	24	25	26	27	28
Week 5	29	30	31	32	33	34	35
Week 6	36	37	38	39	40	41	42

LIVE IN HIS LOVE!

WEEK 2

You're Not Alone

[ISOLATION]

DAY 8

We live in a world that makes it easier and easier to isolate ourselves. We can feel like we're the only ones going through difficult stuff. It was never supposed to be that way.

PRESS PAUSE ⏸ **BETWEEN QUESTIONS**
to reflect and write your answers.

Relax ⏸ PRESS ⏸

Think about how much time you spend alone throughout an average day. Ask God to help you see the need for others in your life and their need for you.

Read ACTS 2:42–47

"All the believers were together and had everything in common."

—*Luke, describing the early Christian church*

Relate | STEP INTO THIS PASSAGE OF SCRIPTURE

For a few moments, really try to get an understanding of the teaching and how it applies to your life.

1. Visualize this passage for a moment. Try to think of these people looking as you look, your same age, and from your same town. Why do you think it was important to go to church together, eat meals together, serve others together, and celebrate together?

2. Can you imagine living around a group of people who had "all things in common"? What would that be like?

3. If you had a group like this to hang out with most of the time, how would your life be different?

4. According to this passage, what was the result of this way of life? Check out verse 47 if you're not sure.

ReACT

In the movie To Save A Life, Roger felt alone and didn't know where to turn. What Roger needed was someone to tell him that he did matter, that he was loved, and there was a God who cared deeply for him.

5. Take a minute to write down a number, on a scale of 1 to 10, that shows how lonely or isolated you've felt lately ("1" being "as lonely as it gets" and "10" being "not lonely at all").

6. Write down your response to a God who promises "to never leave you or forsake you."

If you have an opportunity this week, tell someone that they matter, that their life is important to you and to God.

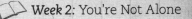

HEY—
ONE LAST THING...

The irony of this lesson is that you are listening to this MP3, learning and reflecting by yourself. This is good, but you can also share how you are growing with others. Find a way to reach out to someone this week. Share your *Devo2Go* with a friend. Talk to them about what it means to you and what it could mean to them.

SHOW LOVE

YOUR PRAYERS + THOUGHTS

You're on **DAY 8** of your journey. Check off each day as you complete it.

Week 1	1	2	3	4	5	6	7
Week 2	8	9	10	11	12	13	14
Week 3	15	16	17	18	19	20	21
Week 4	22	23	24	25	26	27	28
Week 5	29	30	31	32	33	34	35
Week 6	36	37	38	39	40	41	42

YOU ARE NOT ALONE!

[AWARENESS]
DAY 9

When we have a healthy view of ourselves, we're able to start looking more closely at others. A world of hurting people is just waiting to be noticed.

PRESS PAUSE ⏸ **BETWEEN QUESTIONS** to reflect and write your answers.

Relax   PRESS ⏸

Take a moment to rid your mind of any labels that people have put on you. Free your mind to think differently about yourself.

Read   1 CORINTHIANS 15:1–11

"But by the grace of God I am what I am, and his grace to me was not without effect."

—*The apostle Paul to the church at Corinth*

Relate   STEP INTO THIS PASSAGE OF SCRIPTURE

For a few moments, really try to get an understanding of the teaching and how it applies to your life.

1. Write down the reminders Paul gives to his fellow Christians. What does he want you to remember about yourself?

2. How does it make you feel knowing that it's God doing the work in your life, not you?

"Grace" means "unmerited or unearned favor." Basically, God loves you because of who He is, not because you are worthy or cool or smart or beautiful or anything else. He loves you because He made you—you're His child. He loves you enough to give up His only Son for you.

3. What do you think Paul means in verse 10 when he says, "But by the grace of God I am what I am, and his grace to me was not without effect"?

ReACT

4. Write down a prayer to God, asking Him to open your eyes so you can see the people He created and loves around you. Ask Him to remind you of your worth each day and give you courage to live in response to the grace that has been freely given to you.

Think about this question as you go along:
What if I made it a habit to look at others around me the way God looks at them, seeing people like Paul did, with different eyes, seeing the lost and lonely as people who matter to God, to whom He wants to bring hope?

HEY—
ONE LAST THING...

There's a whole world of people out there just waiting to be noticed by you today. When you notice them, they will begin to notice something different about you. That something is knowledge deep in your soul that your life is worth the highest price, and God loves you enough to reveal Himself to you.

SHOW LOVE

YOUR PRAYERS + THOUGHTS

Week 1	1	2	3	4	5	6	7
Week 2	8	**9**	10	11	12	13	14
Week 3	15	16	17	18	19	20	21
Week 4	22	23	24	25	26	27	28
Week 5	29	30	31	32	33	34	35
Week 6	36	37	38	39	40	41	42

PEOPLE ARE WAITING TO BE NOTICED!

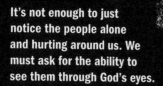

It's not enough to just notice the people alone and hurting around us. We must ask for the ability to see them through God's eyes.

PRESS PAUSE ⏸ BETWEEN QUESTIONS
to reflect and write your answers.

Relax : PRESS ⏸

Take a moment to prepare your mind and heart to think about how you can respond with compassion to the needs around you.

Read : COLOSSIANS 3:12–17

"Clothe yourselves with compassion, kindness, humility, gentleness and patience."

—*The apostle Paul to the church at Colossae*

Relate : STEP INTO THIS PASSAGE OF SCRIPTURE

For a few moments, really try to get an understanding of the teaching and how it applies to your life.

What we find in this passage is a wardrobe description. It tells us that the children of God should have access to certain clothing items every day. Compassion is the first article of clothing that we can't live without.

1. What pain or injustice have you noticed that has caused you to want to change things?

2. Kindness, gentleness, humility, and patience are also pieces of your wardrobe. What parts of this wardrobe do you wear all the time? Do you feel that any of these pieces are missing from your closet? Why or why not?

3. What is your biggest fear in moving beyond just "seeing" other people to actually helping them?

Christ spent His life responding to the needs of the hurting and lonely. When you respond to others' pain or injustice, you do it in the name of Christ. Ask God to help you not only see the needs around you, but also to have the courage to actively seek help for those who struggle.

ReACT

Make it a point today to not only "see" people in need but to intentionally think of ways you might be able to help them or answer their prayers.

4. Who do you see every day who could use an encouraging word or a friend? Remember to see, feel (God will give you compassion) and then do something.

HEY— ONE LAST THING...

Responding with compassion could mean finding help for others in need. Did you ever think that YOU could be the answer to someone's prayers? Tomorrow, we'll take some time to consider the gifts God has given you and how these gifts match up with the needs around you.

SHOW LOVE

YOUR PRAYERS + THOUGHTS

Week 1	1	2	3	4	5	6	7
Week 2	8	9	**10**	11	12	13	14
Week 3	15	16	17	18	19	20	21
Week 4	22	23	24	25	26	27	28
Week 5	29	30	31	32	33	34	35
Week 6	36	37	38	39	40	41	42

YOU COULD BE THE ANSWER TO A PRAYER!

[MISSION]
DAY '11

We're not called to do everything, but we are supposed to do what we can. How do the passions and abilities God has given you match up with the needs that surround you?

PRESS PAUSE ⏸ BETWEEN QUESTIONS
to reflect and write your answers.

[34]

Relax : PRESS ⏸

Begin to think about some of your passions and abilities. God wants to use you, just as you are, to begin changing the world one need at a time.

Read : 1 PETER 4:7–11

"Each of you should use whatever gift you have received to serve others…"

—*The apostle Peter*

Relate : STEP INTO THIS PASSAGE OF SCRIPTURE

For a few moments, really try to get an understanding of the teaching and how it applies to your life.

1. Verse 10 tells us to use whatever gift we have "as a faithful steward of God's grace in its various forms." How does it make you feel to know that God has put us in charge of different types of grace?

2. Write down a few of your talents, skills, and passions. If you can't think of anything, think about the things that make you most happy. This list can help you identify your gifts.

ReAct

3. God has given us this mission in life: to love each other as if our life depended on it. List some specific ways you might use your abilities to love others and to reach out to those who are hurting.

Sharing our gifts with others can make us feel vulnerable, like people will see the person we really are. But God can give us strength and courage, especially when we remember that He called us to love each other.

4. Write a prayer to God asking for His help in using your passions and abilities to meet the needs of others around you.

HEY–
ONE LAST THING...

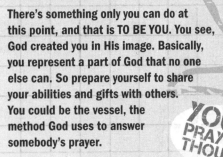

There's something only you can do at this point, and that is TO BE YOU. You see, God created you in His image. Basically, you represent a part of God that no one else can. So prepare yourself to share your abilities and gifts with others. You could be the vessel, the method God uses to answer somebody's prayer.

YOUR PRAYERS + THOUGHTS

Week 1	1	2	3	4	5	6	7
Week 2	8	9	10	*11*	12	13	14
Week 3	15	16	17	18	19	20	21
Week 4	22	23	24	25	26	27	28
Week 5	29	30	31	32	33	34	35
Week 6	36	37	38	39	40	41	42

BE YOURSELF!

[DESPERATE]
DAY '12

You can do a lot of things after you pray...but you can't do anything before you pray. We are completely desperate for God to show up and use our actions to help those around us.

Relax : PRESS ⏸

"Trust in the Lord with all your heart and lean not on your own understanding. In all your ways submit to Him, and He will make your paths straight." As best you know how, seek God with your mind and your heart for a few moments.

Read : EPHESIANS 6:18–20

"Be alert and always keep on praying for all the Lord's people."

—*The apostle Paul to the Ephesians*

Relate : STEP INTO THIS PASSAGE OF SCRIPTURE

For a few moments, really try to get an understanding of the teaching and how it applies to your life.

1. There's a theme in Paul's words; they're calling us to do something. What is he calling us to do?

God loves people, and He especially cares about the people who need help. He loves people so much, He was willing to let Jesus suffer and die for them. So we fearlessly declare this message every time we serve someone or do something with that same type of bold, generous love. By our actions, we're agreeing with God that people matter, and we're agreeing with His message of love.

PRESS PAUSE ⏸ BETWEEN QUESTIONS
to reflect and write your answers.

2. Do you feel like you have what it takes to fearlessly declare the gospel with your actions each day? Why or why not?

ReACT

Chances are you feel a bit inadequate. You may feel like you don't have what it takes to help people around you. We all feel this way sometimes. But this is why we pray.

3. Take some time and ask God to use your life and give you great courage and hope. Say everything you are feeling—God can take it! Write down some of what you're praying below.

HEY—
ONE LAST THING...

Paul ended his letter to the Ephesians by saying, "Grace to all who love our Lord Jesus Christ with an undying love." May you have an undying love for Jesus as you look for ways to be His hands and feet in your home, school, community, and with your friends.

SHOW LOVE

YOUR PRAYERS + THOUGHTS

Week 1	1	2	3	4	5	6	7
Week 2	8	9	10	11	*12*	13	14
Week 3	15	16	17	18	19	20	21
Week 4	22	23	24	25	26	27	28
Week 5	29	30	31	32	33	34	35
Week 6	36	37	38	39	40	41	42

Get the latest on Brooklyn
@ BrooklynLindsey.BlogSpot.com

PRAY TO BE FEARLESS!

DAY '13

Jesus taught that our "neighbor" is anyone who is in need. So many people around the world are hurting and oppressed, and God has given us an opportunity to befriend them—regardless of distance or how different they seem from us.

For Tomorrow...

ON DAY 14, take the opportunity to go to church, attend your youth group, or pray and review this week's devotions.

PRESS PAUSE ⏸ BETWEEN QUESTIONS
to reflect and write your answers.

Relax ⋮ PRESS ⏸

Take a minute to quiet yourself and ask God what He wants to teach you today.

Read ⋮ MATTHEW 25:35–45

"Truly I tell you, whatever you did for one of the least of these brothers and sisters of mine, you did for me."

—*Jesus, speaking to His disciples*

Relate ⋮ STEP INTO THIS PASSAGE OF SCRIPTURE

For a few moments, really try to get an understanding of the teaching and how it applies to your life.

1. When we reach out to someone, befriend them, and meet a need, it's as though we're doing this to Jesus. How does this way of thinking change the way you might view someone who is hungry or homeless?

2. How does the thought of being a friend to someone who is desperately poor, or someone who is seriously sick, or someone who is imprisoned make you feel?

There's a really cool passage in Isaiah 58:7-10. Basically, it says that if we spend ourselves on behalf of the poor—help slaves go free and provide shelter for the wanderer—that our light will shine brightly.

3. Have you felt like your light or witness for Christ has been a little dim? If so, how do you think living out the passage from Matthew and the one from Isaiah might change that?

ReACT

4. Is there an area of need in your community or an issue of suffering in the world in which you feel God may want you to get involved? What can you do to get started?

5. If you're already serving in an area of passion for the poor or hurting, ask God to help you see deeper into the needs of those you're working with. Ask Him to show you how you can demonstrate His love and compassion to others in a new way. Take a minute and write out that prayer.

6. God views your service to the poor and needy as an offering (a gift) to Him. Why do you think He sees it that way? Which of the scripture verses we read today confirms this?

HEY–
ONE LAST THING...

SHOW LOVE

It's important to know that nothing we do for God will increase or decrease His love for us. God IS love. It's His character. He wants us to receive His love ourselves, and then He wants us to be the carriers of His love to a hurting world. It is said that the world will know that God is good if His children show kindness to the poor and hurting.

YOUR PRAYERS + THOUGHTS

Week 1	1	2	3	4	5	6	7
Week 2	8	9	10	11	12	**13**	14
Week 3	15	16	17	18	19	20	21
Week 4	22	23	24	25	26	27	28
Week 5	29	30	31	32	33	34	35
Week 6	36	37	38	39	40	41	42

BE A CARRIER GOD'S LOVE!

WEEK 3
Say Something...Do Something

[HEARTBEAT]

DAY '15

The Holy Spirit will show you when and where you are to move. The more we are in step with God, the better we can see the many opportunities He gives us each day.

Relax : PRESS ⏸

Go ahead, push Pause and ask God to fill you.

Read : ACTS 1:8

"But you will receive power
when the Holy Spirit comes on
you; and you will be my witnesses…"

—*Jesus to His followers*

Relate : STEP INTO THIS PASSAGE OF SCRIPTURE

For a few moments, really try to get an understanding of the teaching and how it applies to your life.

1. What do you think it means to "receive power"? What would you say it means in the context of this passage?

2. Have you ever known someone who was like Jake in the movie *To Save A Life*, when he stood up in youth group? Someone who was bold, courageous and empowered? Who? What did that person do that stood out?

PRESS PAUSE ⏸ BETWEEN QUESTIONS
to reflect and write your answers.

3. The verse we just read was the very last thing Jesus said to His disciples before He was taken up into heaven. Of everything Jesus could have said to them, why do you think He chose this? What impact do you think His words had on the disciples?

ReACT

4. Think about what it might mean to reach out to the lost and lonely on your school campus or in your neighborhood. What do you think you could do on your own (if anything) without God's help or God's power?

5. God promises to help us when we pray and show our willingness to follow Him. What do you think you could do with God's power behind you?

6. Are you trying to do this thing called life on your own? Are you trying to make things happen in your own power? Just for today, consider taking Jesus up on His offer. Plug yourself into His power by telling Him you are powerless on your own.

SHOW LOVE

HEY— ONE LAST THING...

You are different from most people! There is no one else just like you. **BE YOU TODAY** while allowing God's power to speak through all that you do. I dare you to listen to *Devo2Go*™ every day this week!

YOUR PRAYERS + THOUGHTS

You're on **DAY 15** of your journey. Check off each day as you complete it.

Week 1	1	2	3	4	5	6	7
Week 2	8	9	10	11	12	13	14
Week 3	15	16	17	18	19	20	21
Week 4	22	23	24	25	26	27	28
Week 5	29	30	31	32	33	34	35
Week 6	36	37	38	39	40	41	42

PLUG YOURSELF INTO GOD'S POWER!

[43]

(RISK)

DAY '16

It takes guts to open up and admit you're not perfect, and your life's not perfect. When we are honest and open, we give permission for others to do the same.

PRESS PAUSE ⏸ BETWEEN QUESTIONS
to reflect and write your answers.

[44]

Relax : PRESS ⏸

Take a moment to quiet your mind and prepare for this story.

Read : MATTHEW 14:22–32

"Take courage! It is I. Don't be afraid."

—*Jesus to His disciples*

Relax : STEP INTO THIS PASSAGE OF SCRIPTURE

For a few moments, really try to get an understanding of the teaching and how it applies to your life.

1. Why do you think this is one of the most popular Bible stories told?

2. Think of a time when you were scared out of your mind to do something, but you knew you needed to do it because it was the right thing. What was it that you needed to do? Now, think of this—Jesus invites you to step toward that fear, not away from it. Why do you think He does this?

ReACT

3. Which of the following might need to be done in your life? **(Circle one or more.)** If none apply, add your own thought:

A *Reach out to someone unpopular*

B *Break ties with friends who make poor choices*

C *Share honestly about how you feel with a family member(s)*

D *Something else you know you need to do:*

E *Add your own thought(s):*

4. What is one step you can take today that would feel risky, but *right* in the sight of God?

HEY–
ONE LAST THING...

SHOW LOVE

In this story, Jesus invites Peter to step smack-down into his fear and trust Him. And what does Peter do? He steps out. He gets out of the boat. What a stud! Yeah, sure, he sinks after a while, but when he had problems, Jesus was right there to help him. Peter was the apostle who risked.

YOUR PRAYERS + THOUGHTS

Week 1	1	2	3	4	5	6	7
Week 2	8	9	10	11	12	13	14
Week 3	15	**16**	17	18	19	20	21
Week 4	22	23	24	25	26	27	28
Week 5	29	30	31	32	33	34	35
Week 6	36	37	38	39	40	41	42

WILL YOU TAKE A RISK?

[45]

[REJECTION]
DAY '17

We live in a guarded world of people who are quick to be skeptical and slow to trust. Your first acts of kindness might be answered with rejection.

PRESS PAUSE 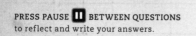 **BETWEEN QUESTIONS** to reflect and write your answers.

Relax : PRESS ⏸

Invite Christ into this moment right now. Would you release your "stuff" to Him? Then, ask God to give you His eyes to see, His ears to hear, and His wisdom to understand.

Read : 1 PETER 4:12–16

"If you are insulted because of the name of Christ, you are blessed."

—*The Apostle Peter*

Relate : STEP INTO THIS PASSAGE OF SCRIPTURE

For a few moments, really try to get an understanding of the teaching and how it applies to your life.

1. In the movie *To Save A Life*, Jake became bold for Christ on his school campus and in his new youth group. He made a risky stand that could have led to rejection. Why do you think he did that?

2. Picture yourself taking the same stand Jake did: standing up in the middle of youth group, telling your new friends to make a difference by reaching out to the lost, lonely, and broken on their school campus. What if people just looked at you with blank stares? How would you feel? Scared? Excited? Fearful?

ReACT

3. When was the last time you were bold about being a Christian? Bold to the point of possible rejection?

4. How bold are you in comparison to Peter? How about in comparison to Christ Himself? Rate your boldness on a scale of 1-10, with 1 being not bold at all and 10 being like Jesus.

5. Who do you know right now who inspires you to make a stand to do the right thing? What about them inspires you?

HEY—
ONE LAST THING...

SHOW LOVE

Many will reject you the first, second, or even third time you make a stand for Christ. But remember, you are in good company! Jesus stands right beside you when you make a stand for Him. And who knows, maybe you will be the one to plant a seed in someone's heart!

YOUR PRAYERS + THOUGHTS

Week 1	1	2	3	4	5	6	7
Week 2	8	9	10	11	12	13	14
Week 3	15	16	**17**	18	19	20	21
Week 4	22	23	24	25	26	27	28
Week 5	29	30	31	32	33	34	35
Week 6	36	37	38	39	40	41	42

Be **BOLD. TAKE A STAND!** [47]

[PERSEVERANCE]
DAY '18

It's not about us doing our "good deed" for the day. It's about coming alongside the hurting and being a friend, even when it's difficult.

Relax : PRESS ⏸

Take one minute to totally quiet your body, your mind, and your heart. Be sure to stop all distractions. Now, say this simple prayer: "God, I need you. God, I want to hear from you. Please be obvious."

Read PHILIPPIANS 3:12–14

"I press on to take hold of that for which Christ Jesus took hold of me."

— *The Apostle Paul to the church at Philippi*

Relax : STEP INTO THIS PASSAGE OF SCRIPTURE

For a few moments, really try to get an understanding of the teaching and how it applies to your life.

1. In this passage, the Apostle Paul refers to Christ taking hold of him. How does it feel when you think about the fact that God chose to "take hold" of you?

2. Remember when we talked about rejection? Rejection can make us reluctant to reach out to people and keep trying. Write down at least one time when you were hurt and it made you hesitate to approach someone.

PRESS PAUSE ⏸ BETWEEN QUESTIONS
to reflect and write your answers.

3. Now, look at verse 13. What would you do differently if you forgot about what was behind (including past hurts) and instead, you chose to "strain toward what is ahead"?

ReACT

In the movie To Save A Life, Jake reached out to the hurting and lonely, even when he initially got no response. At one point, Jake asked Jonny, who was sitting alone at a lunch table, to join his group of friends for lunch. Jonny said no at first. But eventually, Jonny joined them and was better for it, gaining a whole new group of friends.

4. Whom does God want you to press on toward and "hunt" after today? Does someone specific come to mind that you might help? A friend? A family member? A neighbor?

5. What about the lesson from today encourages you to be determined and continue reaching out to the people who have rejected you? What about today's lesson are you going to walk away and apply, as it relates to perseverance?

HEY—
ONE LAST THING...

SHOW LOVE

What did you persevere through this week? Tests? Sports or music competitions? A friend you're trying to reach who keeps rejecting you? Remember, perseverance means "determined continuation; steady and continued action or belief, usually over a long period and especially despite difficulties or setbacks."

YOUR PRAYERS + THOUGHTS

Week 1	1	2	3	4	5	6	7
Week 2	8	9	10	11	12	13	14
Week 3	15	16	17	**18**	19	20	21
Week 4	22	23	24	25	26	27	28
Week 5	29	30	31	32	33	34	35
Week 6	36	37	38	39	40	41	42

WITH GOD'S HELP YOU CAN DO ANYTHING! [49]

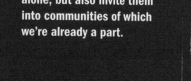

[COOL BY ASSOCIATION]

DAY '19

Community is powerful! We need to not only go into the worlds of those who are alone, but also invite them into communities of which we're already a part.

PRESS PAUSE ▮▮ BETWEEN QUESTIONS to reflect and write your answers.

Relax   PRESS ▮▮

Before jumping into reading the Word, take a deep breath. Now, close your eyes and do that one more time. Let go of whatever brings you stress. Release it into the hands of God this very moment.

Read   ACTS 9:19–28

"But Barnabas took him and brought him to the apostles."

— *Luke, writing about the Apostle Paul*

Relate   STEP INTO THIS PASSAGE OF SCRIPTURE

For a few moments, really try to get an understanding of the teaching and how it applies to your life.

1. What role does Barnabas play in Saul's life and ministry?

2. Barnabas means "Son of Encouragement." (See Acts 4:36.) Name one person (maybe a friend or family member) who is an encouragement to you—someone who acts like Barnabas. (If you don't have one, start praying! We all need a Barnabas!)

ReACT

3. Why do you think God places such importance on living in community?

4. How can you be a Barnabas to someone in your church and/or school? Who comes to mind when you think of someone who is lonely, sad, or depressed? Write down that person's name.

5. What small action can you take to reach out to that person? When will you do this?

HEY—
ONE LAST THING...

YOU are not an accident! God has His hand on your life and wants YOU to live in association with other believers. People (including YOU) matter to God more than anything, and YOU are meant to make a difference and care about them like He does!

SHOW LOVE

YOUR PRAYERS + THOUGHTS

TEAR HERE TO REMOVE YOUR

Week 1	1	2	3	4	5	6	7
Week 2	8	9	10	11	12	13	14
Week 3	15	16	17	18	19	20	21
Week 4	22	23	24	25	26	27	28
Week 5	29	30	31	32	33	34	35
Week 6	36	37	38	39	40	41	42

Learn more about Megan
@ LifeHurtsGodHeals.com

LIVE IN COMMUNITY!

(STUDENT PERSPECTIVE)

DAY 20

With our busy lives, it can be hard to squeeze in time for the things that really matter—like relationships with good friends and with God.

For Tomorrow...

ON DAY 21, take the opportunity to go to church, attend your youth group, or pray and review this week's devotions.

PRESS PAUSE ⏸ BETWEEN QUESTIONS
to reflect and write your answers.

Relax : PRESS ⏸

Take a minute or two and move out of the way anything that might be cluttering your mind. Ask God to open your eyes spiritually to what He might have waiting for you today.

Read : ECCLESIASTES 4:9-10, PROVERBS 13:20, PROVERBS 19:20

"Two are better than one, because they have a good return for their labor."
—*King Solomon*

Relate : STEP INTO THIS PASSAGE OF SCRIPTURE

For a few moments, really try to get an understanding of the teaching and how it applies to your life.

1. I'm sure you've had situations when you were glad you had someone with you who could physically, emotionally, or spiritually pick you up. Describe that situation.

2. Think of a friend or two who might need you right now. How do you think God might want you to work with them, support them, or just be there for them? In the chart below, list some practical things you can do this week to be a supportive friend.

Friend's Name	What I can do this week to show my friendship...

3. What is the hardest thing about taking a risk and reaching out to someone new?

ReACT

4. Are there any risks in making friends who are more spiritually mature than you? What are the risks and the benefits?

God doesn't intend for us to walk through life alone. He's left us here to support and encourage one another. It's amazing that He calls us His "friends." We need to be deliberate about growing our friendship with God in the same way we're deliberate about growing our friendships with other people.

5. What can you move around in your schedule so that you can free up time to spend with God? What might you be doing in your life that could be time better used developing this friendship?

HEY— ONE LAST THING...

SHOW LOVE

In the Bible we're told that God is a friend who sticks closer than a brother. He loves us unconditionally. Unlike our human friends, He's never too busy for us. When you want to spend time with God, He never considers whether He'll get a better offer from someone else. God is investing deeply in your relationship with Him; return the favor!

YOUR PRAYERS + THOUGHTS

Week 1	1	2	3	4	5	6	7
Week 2	8	9	10	11	12	13	14
Week 3	15	16	17	18	19	**20**	21
Week 4	22	23	24	25	26	27	28
Week 5	29	30	31	32	33	34	35
Week 6	36	37	38	39	40	41	42

INVEST IN YOUR RELATIONSHIP WITH GOD!

WEEK 4

What's Your Logline?

[REWRITING STORIES]

DAY 22

We get to go into the worlds of those who are hurting and rewrite who they are according to God and to us.

Relax | PRESS

Take some time right now to put away all the distractions and focus your heart on God. Ask God to open your ears so you can hear His voice speak through this passage.

Read | ACTS 26:4–18

"I have appeared to you to appoint you as a servant and as a witness of what you have seen and will see of me."

— *Jesus to the Apostle Paul*

Relate | STEP INTO THIS PASSAGE OF SCRIPTURE

For a few moments, really try to get an understanding of the teaching and how it applies to your life.

1. Paul had all the religious stuff going, but his heart had become hardened. So much so, that he was destroying the lives of others. Have you seen this happen in your life? Has your heart ever gotten so hard that you've hurt others?

2. How does God soften people's hearts and help them build up, rather than damage, other people?

PRESS PAUSE ❚❚ BETWEEN QUESTIONS
to reflect and write your answers.

[56]

3. We see that Paul had an experience with God's overwhelming love. Have you ever had an encounter with God? What happened?

You can have an experience right now! Just reach out to God and talk to Him like you would talk to your best friend. He'll respond.

ReACT

Paul's story was rewritten that day. He went from killing Christians to being the leader of the Christian church!

4. Are there people in your life who need to be changed? Who and in what ways? Write down a list of a few people, and pray about how God can use you to re-write their stories.

5. Sometime today, if not right now, look back on your walk with God. Make a list of some things God has rewritten in your life. Maybe even during this *Devo2Go*™ series. Is He changing the way you treat others? Or has He given you dreams you never thought you could have?

Remember these things, so you can share them with others and brag on God!

HEY—
ONE LAST THING...

Remember—you may not always feel like it, but God HAS chosen you. He wants you to work with him in rewriting the stories of people who desperately need Him. Let's not wait until tomorrow to put this into action. Why not today?

SHOW LOVE

YOUR PRAYERS + THOUGHTS

You're on **DAY 22** of your journey. Check off each day as you complete it.

Week 1	1	2	3	4	5	6	7
Week 2	8	9	10	11	12	13	14
Week 3	15	16	17	18	19	20	21
Week 4	22	23	24	25	26	27	28
Week 5	29	30	31	32	33	34	35
Week 6	36	37	38	39	40	41	42

REWRITE STORIES WITH GOD! [57]

[SELF IMAGE]
DAY 23

We get to rewrite stories and affect how people think about themselves and how they believe God sees them.

PRESS PAUSE ⏸ BETWEEN QUESTIONS
to reflect and write your answers.

(58)

Relax : PRESS ⏸

Press pause for a moment. Maybe take a deep breath, and quiet any distraction in your mind. Let God's Word really sink in, and open your ears to the whisper of His voice.

Read : MARK 5:1–20

"When they came to Jesus, they saw the man who had been possessed by the legion of demons, sitting there, dressed and in his right mind..."

—*Mark, writing about Jesus' healing of a possessed man*

Relate : STEP INTO THIS PASSAGE OF SCRIPTURE

For a few moments, really try to get an understanding of the teaching and how it applies to your life.

The young possessed man was living in and controlled by death. It says that he LIVED in the tombs!

1. Have you ever been in a dark place? Are you there right now? Why don't you write about that experience, or write a short prayer to God. He can bring you out!

Jesus asked, "What's your name?" The spirits replied back saying, "My name is Legion for we are many." Jesus knew from the beginning that the voice coming out of the young man was NOT him. He knew that the man's current state was not who he really was.

2. Did you ever pretend to be someone or something that you're not? What did you pretend and why?

3. What is YOUR name? Who are you really?

4. Have other people given you a bad definition? Why do you think they did that?

ReACT

The demon-possessed man was totally set free in a dramatic way. The passage says that after his transformation, the man traveled the region proclaiming how much Jesus had done for him. Did you know that your testimony is one of your most powerful weapons? Ask God to give you opportunities today and this week to share your story with others.

4. From what has God set you free? What has He helped you overcome?

SHOW LOVE

HEY— ONE LAST THING...

When we look at our failures, we think that we'll never be good enough. But the whole time Jesus sees HIMSELF in us. When we received Jesus into our hearts and believed in Him, we were made in His likeness! Not only does God love you, but He likes you and wants a real relationship with you.

YOUR PRAYERS + THOUGHTS

Week 1	1	2	3	4	5	6	7
Week 2	8	9	10	11	12	13	14
Week 3	15	16	17	18	19	20	21
Week 4	22	**23**	24	25	26	27	28
Week 5	29	30	31	32	33	34	35
Week 6	36	37	38	39	40	41	42

Sharing YOUR story can help others rewrite theirs!

WHAT'S YOUR REAL NAME?

(REJECTION)
DAY 24

We get to rewrite stories of how people have felt rejected and not good enough. We can let them know they are perfect the way they are.

PRESS PAUSE ❚❚ BETWEEN QUESTIONS
to reflect and write your answers.

[60]

Relax : PRESS ❚❚

Stop for a moment. Prepare your heart to read God's Word. Expect to hear from Him as you dive into this passage.

Read : JOHN 8:1–11

"Let any one of you who is without sin be the first to throw a stone at her."

—Jesus, speaking about a woman accused of adultery

Relate : STEP INTO THIS PASSAGE OF SCRIPTURE

For a few moments, really try to get an understanding of the teaching and how it applies to your life.

1. The crowd was so quick to want this woman punished. Have you ever done that before? Have you ever picked up a stone before thinking about it or examining your own heart?

2. Jesus saw something in her that the people didn't see. Did He focus on her sin or on her potential to be FREE from sin? What makes you think that?

If you have judged others, take the time to repent, which means to openly admit your mistakes, turn away from them, and walk in the other direction. Make a commitment to change and ask God to help you see the best in everyone.

ReACT

3. Jesus was willing to stand up for a person whom everyone hated. Are there people at your school who are disliked or judged?

4. What are some ways you could stand up for those people and show them love?

HEY— ONE LAST THING...

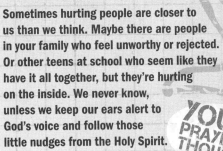

SHOW LOVE

Sometimes hurting people are closer to us than we think. Maybe there are people in your family who feel unworthy or rejected. Or other teens at school who seem like they have it all together, but they're hurting on the inside. We never know, unless we keep our ears alert to God's voice and follow those little nudges from the Holy Spirit.

YOUR PRAYERS + THOUGHTS

Week 1	1	2	3	4	5	6	7
Week 2	8	9	10	11	12	13	14
Week 3	15	16	17	18	19	20	21
Week 4	22	23	**24**	25	26	27	28
Week 5	29	30	31	32	33	34	35
Week 6	36	37	38	39	40	41	42

STAND UP FOR SOMEONE BEING JUDGED !

[GUILT]
DAY 25

We get to rewrite stories in which people have been carrying around the weight of a past regret. Introduce them to freedom through God's grace.

Relax : PRESS **❚❚**

Press pause, remove every distraction, and let God's Word speak loud and clear.

Read : JOHN 21:15–19

"Jesus said, 'Take care of my sheep.'"

—*Jesus to the Apostle Peter*

Relate : STEP INTO THIS PASSAGE OF SCRIPTURE

For a few moments, really try to get an understanding of the teaching and how it applies to your life.

1. Why do you think Jesus asked Peter this question three times in a row?

2. Are you carrying around any guilt? Why? What caused it?

3. Has guilt ever stopped you from doing something for someone else? From feeling good about yourself?

4. Judging from how Jesus reacted to Peter, what do you think God wants you to do with your guilt?

ReACT

5. If you've struggled with guilt, you know how terrible it feels. Is there anything holding you back from helping others be free? If so, what is it?

6. Do you know people who need God's freedom from guilt and shame? Write down a few names, and begin to pray for them. Then ask God for opportunities to remind them that God loves them and has completely forgiven them!

If they've never experienced God's forgiveness, tell the amazing news about what Jesus has done. By dying on the cross, He broke us out of our prison cells forever. With God's help, you'll rewrite their story.

HEY— ONE LAST THING...

SHOW LOVE

We've discussed four different topics already this week. Take the time to scan them again. Look at this whole week as a big picture and ask God to really drive that picture home. Tomorrow, we'll look at how we can rewrite the stories of people who struggle with greed.

YOUR PRAYERS + THOUGHTS

Week 1	1	2	3	4	5	6	7
Week 2	8	9	10	11	12	13	14
Week 3	15	16	17	18	19	20	21
Week 4	22	23	24	*25*	26	27	28
Week 5	29	30	31	32	33	34	35
Week 6	36	37	38	39	40	41	42

REWRITE STORIES OF GUILT! [63]

(GREED)

DAY 26

We get to rewrite stories that have been self-centered and show others the power and joy in sacrificial giving.

Relax | PRESS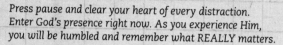

Press pause and clear your heart of every distraction. Enter God's presence right now. As you experience Him, you will be humbled and remember what REALLY matters.

Read : LUKE 19:1–10

"Look, Lord! Here and now I give half of my possessions to the poor..."

—*Zacchaeus to Jesus*

Relate | STEP INTO THIS PASSAGE OF SCRIPTURE

For a few moments, really try to get an understanding of the teaching and how it applies to your life.

1. Zacchaeus must have had quite the bad reputation. He had been in the middle of a lot of bad business deals and took advantage of a lot of people. His bank account was full of dirty money. So, why do you think Jesus picked him, out of all the people in the crowd?

2. It seems like Zacchaeus was a very greedy person. What do you think happened in those moments with Jesus that caused such a radical change?

PRESS PAUSE  BETWEEN QUESTIONS
to reflect and write your answers.

3. Can you relate to any part of this story? Like Zacchaeus, do you sometimes expect less for yourself—thinking all you want is more and more stuff and it's never enough? How does that thinking affect you?

4. What about this story illustrates that God has only the best for YOU?

ReACT

Jesus rewrote Zacchaeus's story that day. It changed the course of his life.

5. Are there people in your life who struggle with greed? How should you approach them? Does anything in this story help you?

HEY— ONE LAST THING...

When we look into the face of God, material things start to seem really silly. As we draw close to Him, our stories will be rewritten. Find someone today and discuss this with them. Have a conversation about your priorities and talk about how you both can put God first.

SHOW LOVE

YOUR PRAYERS + THOUGHTS

Week 1	1	2	3	4	5	6	7
Week 2	8	9	10	11	12	13	14
Week 3	15	16	17	18	19	20	21
Week 4	22	23	24	25	**26**	27	28
Week 5	29	30	31	32	33	34	35
Week 6	36	37	38	39	40	41	42

Visit Leeland and enjoy their music @ LeelandOnline.com

IT'S ABOUT GOD. NOT STUFF!

[65]

STUDENT PERSPECTIVE

DAY 27

This week we've been looking at rewriting stories. Let's continue that idea and look at the next chapter in your story, or **THE NEW STORY.**

For Tomorrow...

ON DAY 28, take the opportunity to go to church, attend your youth group, or pray and review this week's devotions.

PRESS PAUSE ❚❚ BETWEEN QUESTIONS
to reflect and write your answers.

Relax ❚ PRESS ❚❚

Take a minute to relax, clear away any distractions, and ask God to speak to you through today's devotional.

Read ❙ 2 CORINTHIANS 5:15-21

"Therefore, if anyone is in Christ, the new creation has come: The old has gone, the new is here!"

—*The Apostle Paul, to the church at Corinth*

Relate ❙ STEP INTO THIS PASSAGE OF SCRIPTURE

For a few moments, really try to get an understanding of the teaching and how it applies to your life.

1. Look at the first part of the passage. What does it mean to not regard someone from a worldly point of view?

2. Describe what the "old you" was like.

3. Imagine that the old you has been put to death and a brand-new you has been resurrected like Jesus. How is the new you different? How should the new you be different?

ReACT

4. Verse 20 calls us Christ's "ambassadors." How does an ambassador who loves God and loves people appear to those who are living in the world?

5. When you love people this way, how will it affect their view of Christ? How can your love draw people to God?

HEY— ONE LAST THING...

SHOW LOVE

God wants to use us to rewrite the story of the world. He could easily manipulate every circumstance—end all of the suffering, make everyone happy—with just a snap of His fingers. But God doesn't want to do that; He wants to be with us, to work with us, because He loves us. God is our loving Father, and wants to let us help Him change the world.

YOUR PRAYERS + THOUGHTS

Week 1	1	2	3	4	5	6	7
Week 2	8	9	10	11	12	13	14
Week 3	15	16	17	18	19	20	21
Week 4	22	23	24	25	26	**27**	28
Week 5	29	30	31	32	33	34	35
Week 6	36	37	38	39	40	41	42

LET GOD'S LOVE SHINE THROUGH YOU!

WEEK 5

How To Save A Life

(LEARN TO LISTEN)
DAY 29

The best conversationalists are those who know how to ask good questions and then just listen. People are literally dying to be heard.

Relax : PRESS ⏸

Press pause and quiet your mind. For a moment, just listen to what you hear around you. If you don't quiet your heart and mind, you may actually miss what God is whispering to you.

Read : JAMES 1:19–21

"Everyone should be quick to listen, slow to speak and slow to become angry..."

—James, church leader and brother of Jesus

Relate : STEP INTO THIS PASSAGE OF SCRIPTURE

Have you ever said something to your parents, and then wished you hadn't said it? Or thrown out a comment to a friend, and then wished you could take it back? Maybe a friend was trying to tell you something about themselves, and you "jumped to conclusions," which resulted in a misunderstanding or even anger.

1. Have you been quick to speak, but a few seconds later wished you hadn't said something? What happened?

2. When we are told to be quick to listen, what do you think "listen" actually means? How can you listen, other than just using your ears?

PRESS PAUSE ⏸ BETWEEN QUESTIONS
to reflect and write your answers.

ReACT

3. There will be many times, probably even today, when someone is talking and you will want to answer them right away. You might even start thinking about what you are going to say before they finish talking, rather than paying attention to what they are trying to communicate. Write down the last time you remember doing that.

4. When you did do that, how do you think it affected the conversation? How might the discussion have gone differently if you were listening carefully?

Today, after a friend or parent shares something with you, try repeating it back to them by saying, "I think I hear you saying…" This is called active listening, and it shows your heart to really understand them rather than just make your point. It's also a great way to communicate value to others. Another thing you can do is think, "How does this person make me feel?" This helps you listen better.

HEY— ONE LAST THING...

SHOW LOVE

Listening is not always easy. Give the other person a chance—try to understand what they are really saying, not just what the words are. You have been listening to these devos for 29 days, and that shows you are learning how to listen— keep it up!

YOUR PRAYERS + THOUGHTS

You're on **DAY 29** of your journey. Check off each day as you complete it.

Week 1	1	2	3	4	5	6	7
Week 2	8	9	10	11	12	13	14
Week 3	15	16	17	18	19	20	21
Week 4	22	23	24	25	26	27	28
Week 5	29	30	31	32	33	34	35
Week 6	36	37	38	39	40	41	42

COMMIT TO BEING A BETTER LISTENER!

(SEEING THE BEST IN PEOPLE)

DAY 30

If you are truly going to make a difference in someone's life, you need to see the best in people.

PRESS PAUSE ⏸ BETWEEN QUESTIONS
to reflect and write your answers.

[72]

Relax : PRESS ⏸

Take a moment to identify the distractions around you (turn off that TV, maybe close the blinds, go into a quiet room if possible) and in your mind (stop worrying about that test, game, or plan for Friday). Ask God to speak to you as you go through today's devotional.

Read : MATTHEW 26:6–13, 1 SAMUEL 16:7

"People look at the outward appearance, but the Lord looks at the heart."

—God to the prophet Samuel

Relate : STEP INTO THIS PASSAGE OF SCRIPTURE

For a few moments, really try to get an understanding of the teaching and how it applies to your life.

1. Have you ever met someone and made assumptions about them based on what you saw on the outside, and then later learned you did not really understand them or know them? Describe a time when that happened.

Sometimes, people put up defenses or act a certain way based on hurts they have experienced in the past. They might be hiding behind a "front."

2. Do you hide sometimes? Maybe behind clothes, actions, music, or words you speak? Can people know your heart based on your actions? List some ways you might be hiding, and why you think you do it.

3. Have you ever judged someone's actions (like the disciples did in Matthew 26) before really considering what the action meant? Summarize the experience in the space below.

ReACT

4. List one or two people you might be misjudging because you are looking at their outward appearance. How would Jesus treat the people on your list?

Remember the outward appearance does NOT indicate everything that is happening in a person's heart. You have to work to see the best; assume the best about others and give them a chance. Love them with Christ's love in spite of what your first impression might be.

5. Choose someone from the list above and spend one day concentrating on the best in them. Make a point to tell them about it. In short, treat them the way Jesus would treat them.

HEY–
ONE LAST THING...

Really listening will help you see the best in people. Ask questions to get to know people's hearts. It all ties together, so press on!

SHOW LOVE

YOUR PRAYERS + THOUGHTS

Week 1	1	2	3	4	5	6	7
Week 2	8	9	10	11	12	13	14
Week 3	15	16	17	18	19	20	21
Week 4	22	23	24	25	26	27	28
Week 5	29	**30**	31	32	33	34	35
Week 6	36	37	38	39	40	41	42

SEE THE BEST IN PEOPLE!

(REALLY CELEBRATE)
DAY 31

In a world filled with competition, jealousy, and envy, there is something really powerful about truly being happy when someone succeeds. So, *"GO OVER THE TOP"* when you celebrate!

Relax : PRESS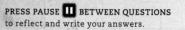

Press pause and focus on what we are going to cover today. Ask God to whisper into your heart as you go though this devotional. Ask Him to challenge you.

Read   PHILIPPIANS 4:4

"Rejoice in the Lord always.
I will say it again: Rejoice!"

—*The Apostle Paul encouraging the Philippians*

Relax : STEP INTO THIS PASSAGE OF SCRIPTURE

For a few moments, really try to get an understanding of the teaching and how it applies to your life.

1. What is the difficulty in "rejoicing always"? Would you say it's even possible to rejoice always? Why or why not?

2. Do you think there's a difference between "rejoicing" and being "happy"? If so, what is the difference?

PRESS PAUSE ❚❚ BETWEEN QUESTIONS
to reflect and write your answers.

In Philippians 2:4, the Apostle Paul says, "Each of you should look not only to your own interests, but also to the interests of others."

3. What is typically your first reaction when someone you know succeeds—are you excited for them, or do you wish it had happened to you?

4. Think of a time when you had a really great success, or when something great happened to you. What happened when you told people about it? How did their reaction make you feel?

5. Describe a time when you "rejoiced" in something you saw God do, in your life or in someone else's life.

ReACT

Sometimes we start to think about how we would like good things to happen to us rather than celebrate the win for our friends. Clearly, we are challenged in Philippians to get excited with them and to watch out for their interests.

6. What is your reaction going to be the next time a friend comes and shares with you their really great news?

HEY—
ONE LAST THING...

Today, FIND things to celebrate in others' lives. Go out of your way to find people and celebrate them. Make others the center of attention. You can do this as you listen to them and believe the best about them. Make someone else a hero today!

SHOW LOVE

YOUR PRAYERS + THOUGHTS

Week 1	1	2	3	4	5	6	7
Week 2	8	9	10	11	12	13	14
Week 3	15	16	17	18	19	20	21
Week 4	22	23	24	25	26	27	28
Week 5	29	30	*31*	32	33	34	35
Week 6	36	37	38	39	40	41	42

CELEBRATE WITH GOD!

(REALLY HURT)

DAY 32

I've heard that if a friend tells you a sad story from their life and you cry before they do—they will be your best friend for life. Learn to empathize.

PRESS PAUSE ⏸ BETWEEN QUESTIONS
to reflect and write your answers.

(76)

Relax ⋮ PRESS ⏸

Press pause and again get focused on what we are going to cover here today. Ask God to whisper into your heart as you go though this devotional. Ask Him to challenge you and maybe even break your heart for someone who needs your empathy.

Read ⋮ MATTHEW 26:36–46

"My soul is overwhelmed with sorrow to the point of death. Stay here and keep watch with me."

—Jesus to His apostles, Peter, James and John

Relate ⋮ STEP INTO THIS PASSAGE OF SCRIPTURE

For a few moments, really try to get an understanding of the teaching and how it applies to your life.

1. How do you think Jesus felt when He found his friends sleeping while His own heart was being crushed? How do you think He felt the second time He found them asleep?

2. If you had been there with Jesus, do you think you would have gone to sleep? Why or why not?

3. Who do you go to when you need to "pour out your heart"? Why do you go to that person?

ReACT

4. How can you tell when a friend needs to talk, even if they don't say anything or if they just say, "I'm fine"?

5. What are some specific ways in which you can be "awake" when a friend needs you?

HEY— ONE LAST THING...

SHOW LOVE

Today, really listen as your friends and others are sharing about their lives. They may not say some things out loud, but ask God to give you eyes to see what they are really feeling, ears to hear what they are really saying, and a heart that's filled with empathy as you spend time with your friends today.

YOUR PRAYERS + THOUGHTS

Week 1	1	2	3	4	5	6	7
Week 2	8	9	10	11	12	13	14
Week 3	15	16	17	18	19	20	21
Week 4	22	23	24	25	26	27	28
Week 5	29	30	31	**32**	33	34	35
Week 6	36	37	38	39	40	41	42

STAY "AWAKE" WITH YOUR FRIENDS!

(BE JESUS)
DAY 33

Realize that you may be the closest some people will ever get to seeing Jesus. The word Christian simply means to "BE LIKE CHRIST."

Relax   PRESS

Press pause and remember what we discussed yesterday about really hurting, really empathizing with someone else. Know that God has new places He wants to take you today. Ask Him to take you there, to show you Himself, and to continue to change you.

Read   PHILIPPIANS 2:3–11

"He made himself nothing by taking the very nature of a servant, being made in human likeness."

—*The Apostle Paul, describing Jesus*

Relate   STEP INTO THIS PASSAGE OF SCRIPTURE

For a few moments, really try to get an understanding of the teaching and how it applies to your life.

1. *This passage says that Jesus, who was and is God, did not demand His rights. He allowed Himself to be treated as* **nothing**.

What do you think it was like for Jesus to leave heaven—where He was a holy, revered King—and become human on earth? To take on the sin of mankind, even though He didn't sin at all?

PRESS PAUSE BETWEEN QUESTIONS
to reflect and write your answers.

2. Have you ever said to someone, "Hey, stop talking to me like that; I have a right to be respected"? What happened?

3. Describe a time in which someone gave up their rights for your benefit. What happened and how did that make you feel?

ReACT

4. How can you imitate Christ's humility this week at home? At school? At church?

HEY–
ONE LAST THING...

This is going to be a tough one! As you go through the day today, try to give up all your rights: the right for your little brother to treat you a certain way, the right to be talked to by your friends a certain way, the right to tell your side of the story, etc.

SHOW LOVE

YOUR PRAYERS + THOUGHTS

Week 1	1	2	3	4	5	6	7
Week 2	8	9	10	11	12	13	14
Week 3	15	16	17	18	19	20	21
Week 4	22	23	24	25	26	27	28
Week 5	29	30	31	32	**33**	34	35
Week 6	36	37	38	39	40	41	42

Check out Dave and Teen Mania
@ **TeenMania.com**

HUMBLE YOURSELF!

DAY 34

Jesus was very "OTHERS-CONSCIOUS." He listened well and often asked a question in return rather than making a statement. Today, we'll take a look at some of the ways we're to treat others.

For Tomorrow...

ON DAY 35, take the opportunity to go to church, attend your youth group, or pray and review this week's devotions.

PRESS PAUSE ▮▮ BETWEEN QUESTIONS to reflect and write your answers.

Relax ⋮ PRESS ▮▮

Take a minute to get rid of the stuff that might distract you, so that you can concentrate.

Read ⋮ LUKE 6:27–36

"But to you who are listening I say: Love your enemies, do good to those who hate you..."

— *Jesus, speaking to His disciples and the Jewish crowd*

Relate ⋮ STEP INTO THIS PASSAGE OF SCRIPTURE

For a few moments, really try to get an understanding of the teaching and how it applies to your life.

1. How do you normally react to being mistreated? How does Jesus' teaching differ from our natural reaction to being mistreated?

2. Can you think of an example of when you've seen someone else live out this radical (and counterintuitive) teaching? What happened?

3. In verse 32, Jesus is explaining that because it is so easy to love people who love us, we can't really take credit for being such great and moral people when we express that natural type of love. Now, look at verses 33 through 36. How did Jesus live out what He was asking of us?

ReACT

4. How did Jesus' life on earth enable Him to empathize with us when we have to deal with tough-to-love people?

5. Based on that, how much credibility does Jesus have when He asks us to love our enemies?

6. Go back to verses 27 through 29. Describe a relationship or situation in your life in which you might have the chance to love an "enemy." Name something specific you can do this week.

If you sense this is going to be really hard for you, ask God for help. Ask Him to walk with you and to help you with the right words and attitude to love people who are hard to love. Ask Him to help you see them the way He does. Maybe even write that prayer out in your journal. You can use the space in the lower right corner for your prayers and thoughts.

HEY—
ONE LAST THING...

SHOW LOVE

You might be surprised to find that when you start loving the difficult people in your life, they aren't necessarily the only ones who change. You might be transformed, too. Don't forget to talk with a friend this week about what you've learned; it's easier to walk the road with someone else.

YOUR PRAYERS + THOUGHTS

Week 1	1	2	3	4	5	6	7
Week 2	8	9	10	11	12	13	14
Week 3	15	16	17	18	19	20	21
Week 4	22	23	24	25	26	27	28
Week 5	29	30	31	32	33	**34**	35
Week 6	36	37	38	39	40	41	42

LOVE YOUR ENEMIES!

WEEK 6

Stepping Into the Bigger Story

[THE FIRST CHURCH]

DAY 36

Travel back 2,000 years and step into the story of the early Christian church. What were they devoted to?

PRESS PAUSE **⏸** BETWEEN QUESTIONS
to reflect and write your answers.

Relax : PRESS **⏸**

Put aside any distractions and open your heart to what God wants you to hear from Him.

Read : ACTS 2:42–47

"They devoted themselves to the apostles' teaching and to the fellowship, to the breaking of bread and to prayer."

—*Luke, describing the early Christian church*

Relate : STEP INTO THIS PASSAGE OF SCRIPTURE

For a few moments, really try to get an understanding of the teaching and how it applies to your life.

1. As you've gone through the past few weeks of this *Devo2Go*™ (this is your last week), has your focus changed? Has God moved your heart and connected with you?

2. Write down some ways in which you think God has moved in your heart and changed your attitude toward others.

Maybe for the first time, you are becoming aware of others around you who NEED God in their lives. You see? Your focus has changed.

3. Write down the names of the people you feel God is calling you to reach out to.

ReACT

4. The early believers did specific things to help themselves grow and mature as followers of Christ. Read the passage again. What were the believers devoted to?

5. What can YOU do to help yourself learn about a God-following life?

HEY—
ONE LAST THING...

When you make a decision to walk with God, remember that He will give you the places and the people to help you. Tomorrow we'll look at some things you can do as you learn.

SHOW LOVE

YOUR PRAYERS + THOUGHTS

You're on **DAY 36** of your journey. Check off each day as you complete it.

Week 1	1	2	3	4	5	6	7
Week 2	8	9	10	11	12	13	14
Week 3	15	16	17	18	19	20	21
Week 4	22	23	24	25	26	27	28
Week 5	29	30	31	32	33	34	35
Week 6	36	37	38	39	40	41	42

WHAT ARE YOU DEVOTED TO?

(NO SECRET) DAY 37

The members of the first century church knew where to learn about their new life. They relied on the teaching of the apostles and not on the rumors or opinions of their friends.

PRESS PAUSE  BETWEEN QUESTIONS
to reflect and write your answers.

(86)

Relax : PRESS ⏸

Take a breath. Clear your mind and open your heart to the Lord.

Read   ACTS 2:42–43

"They devoted themselves
  to the _apostles_' teaching…"

—Luke

Relate : STEP INTO THIS PASSAGE OF SCRIPTURE

For a few moments, really try to get an understanding of the teaching and how it applies to your life.

1. What are the benefits of having a place to go to learn how to follow God, instead of just doing it on your own?

2. What would this place have to look like? What aspects of such a place would be most important to you?

ReACT

3. Name some of the people you know who go to church and attend Bible study.

4. Think about the early Christians in the passage we read; they learned from the disciples, who spent three years following Jesus. Who do you know who seems to really know the Bible and have a close relationship with God?

5. Choose one or two of these people who could help you as you keep learning more and more about the Christian life. How will you make time to "hang out" with them? (Think about getting together at home or at school, going places together, meeting regularly just to talk about anything.)

HEY–
ONE LAST THING...

SHOW LOVE

Remember, throughout your life many people will try to influence you, but you need to identify the people you will trust to teach you about God. Tomorrow we will discuss other things you can be doing as you grow in your ability to follow the Lord.

YOUR PRAYERS + THOUGHTS

Week 1	1	2	3	4	5	6	7
Week 2	8	9	10	11	12	13	14
Week 3	15	16	17	18	19	20	21
Week 4	22	23	24	25	26	27	28
Week 5	29	30	31	32	33	34	35
Week 6	36	**37**	38	39	40	41	42

WHO CAN TEACH YOU ABOUT GOD? [87]

(NEVER-ENDING GARAGE SALE)

DAY 38

In the early Christian church, no one was ever in need. The Christians sold their possessions, provided for each other, and gave generously to the poor.

PRESS PAUSE ⏸ **BETWEEN QUESTIONS**
to reflect and write your answers.

Relax ⏸ PRESS ⏸

Take a minute to relax and get focused on God. Now, let's dig into today's devotional.

Read ACTS 2:44–45

"They sold property and possessions to give to anyone who had need."

—Luke's description of the 1st century church

Relate STEP INTO THIS PASSAGE OF SCRIPTURE

What if the first thing you learned was that all of your valuables, your talents, time, and material things have a different purpose—one that is much bigger than the way you currently use them?

1. What would you do if God showed you that He wanted to use your money and your stuff for something else? Would you be willing to let God re-purpose them? Why or why not?

ReACT

2. Imagine you met someone really in need of God's love, and God put it on your heart to give that person something you own? Could you do it? What would you do?

3. Of the stuff you own, what would be the hardest thing to share or give up altogether? Why?

4. If everyone in your "hang out" group committed to sharing their stuff and helping each other, would you join in? What would you contribute? What would you need from them in return?

HEY—
ONE LAST THING...

God doesn't want to take away your stuff. But He sometimes asks you to contribute to a much bigger purpose than your own pleasure and comfort. Living a generous life is one of the many ways we show God that we love and trust Him. It's also a way we can show His love to others.

SHOW LOVE

YOUR PRAYERS + THOUGHTS

Week 1	1	2	3	4	5	6	7
Week 2	8	9	10	11	12	13	14
Week 3	15	16	17	18	19	20	21
Week 4	22	23	24	25	26	27	28
Week 5	29	30	31	32	33	34	35
Week 6	36	37	*38*	39	40	41	42

LIVE A
GENEROUS LIFE!

[EVERYDAY SUNDAY]
DAY 39

The early church met together every single day, and not just at church, but in their homes as well. Imagine what your life would look like if you chose to hang out with God 24/7.

PRESS PAUSE ⏸ BETWEEN QUESTIONS
to reflect and write your answers.

Relax : PRESS ⏸

Take a moment, relax, and ask God to reveal His desire for your life.

Read : ACTS 2:46

"Every day they continued to meet together in the temple courts."
—Luke

Relate : STEP INTO THIS PASSAGE OF SCRIPTURE

For a few moments, really try to get an understanding of the teaching and how it applies to your life.

1. What do you devote yourself to *every day*? Where do you spend most of your time, attention, and money? List the top three things below.

2. Why do you think the early church met *every day*?

3. Why do you think it was important for them to learn the rules of their new life *really fast*?

3. Of the stuff you own, what would be the hardest thing to share or give up altogether? Why?

4. If everyone in your "hang out" group committed to sharing their stuff and helping each other, would you join in? What would you contribute? What would you need from them in return?

HEY— ONE LAST THING...

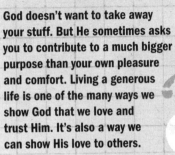

SHOW LOVE

God doesn't want to take away your stuff. But He sometimes asks you to contribute to a much bigger purpose than your own pleasure and comfort. Living a generous life is one of the many ways we show God that we love and trust Him. It's also a way we can show His love to others.

YOUR PRAYERS + THOUGHTS

Week 1	1	2	3	4	5	6	7
Week 2	8	9	10	11	12	13	14
Week 3	15	16	17	18	19	20	21
Week 4	22	23	24	25	26	27	28
Week 5	29	30	31	32	33	34	35
Week 6	36	37	*38*	39	40	41	42

LIVE A GENEROUS LIFE!

[EVERYDAY SUNDAY]
DAY 39

The early church met together every single day, and not just at church, but in their homes as well. Imagine what your life would look like if you chose to hang out with God 24/7.

PRESS PAUSE ❚❚ BETWEEN QUESTIONS to reflect and write your answers.

Relax ❚❚ PRESS ❚❚

Take a moment, relax, and ask God to reveal His desire for your life.

Read ACTS 2:46

"Every day they continued to meet together in the temple courts."

—Luke

Relate STEP INTO THIS PASSAGE OF SCRIPTURE

For a few moments, really try to get an understanding of the teaching and how it applies to your life.

1. What do you devote yourself to *every day*? Where do you spend most of your time, attention, and money? List the top three things below.

2. Why do you think the early church met *every day*?

3. Why do you think it was important for them to learn the rules of their new life *really fast*?

4. If you'd been invited to join this early church, how would you have felt about it? What do you like about the idea? What do you think would take some getting used to? What would be difficult?

ReACT

5. The Bible says that whatever you commit most of your resources to—your time, your attention, your money—that's where your heart will be. How much of your resources do you put into learning more about God, serving other people, and getting together with other believers?

6. What do you think you can do to hang out with God more often? How can you improve the quality and quantity of your experiences with God?

7. You're almost done with this *Devo2Go*™. What you are going to do next? Write down some action steps.

SHOW LOVE

HEY–
ONE LAST THING...

Walking with God requires that you learn new skills. You now know that it's not hard to get that learning. And, you know **WHERE** to get it.

YOUR PRAYERS + THOUGHTS

Week 1	1	2	3	4	5	6	7
Week 2	8	9	10	11	12	13	14
Week 3	15	16	17	18	19	20	21
Week 4	22	23	24	25	26	27	28
Week 5	29	30	31	32	33	34	35
Week 6	36	37	38	**39**	40	41	42

HOW DO YOU SPEND YOUR TIME & MONEY? [91]

[SCOOT OVER]

DAY 40

The Christian community is not just for you and your friends; the coolest parties always attract people. So scoot over and make room for more!

PRESS PAUSE ⏸ BETWEEN QUESTIONS
to reflect and write your answers.

Relax : PRESS ⏸

Take a minute to prepare your heart and mind for today's devotional.

Read   ACTS 2:47

"And the Lord added to their number daily those who were being saved."

—*Luke, writing about the early church*

Relate : STEP INTO THIS PASSAGE OF SCRIPTURE

For a few moments, really try to get an understanding of the teaching and how it applies to your life.

1. How is this description like or unlike the fellowship you enjoy with your youth group (or other group of believers)? How could you help your group be more like the early church?

2. How does being involved in a Christian group, spending time with other people, and learning how to live for God benefit the whole group, including you?

3. If you are actively part of a Christian group enjoying this new "party" and learning, growing, and enjoying God together—what could this mean for a newcomer?

4. What do you think the group (including you) believes about their new lives? Do you ever tell anybody else how cool being "saved" is? Why or why not?

ReACT

5. Do you ever tell anybody how loving your community of friends is? Why or why not?

6. What can each of the members of your group do to meet the needs of newcomers?

7. Think about all those who haven't yet discovered God's love and power in their lives. What do you think might happen to them if you don't tell them that God wants to heal their hurts?

8. Name one person you should tell about your relationship with God. Why did you choose that person? What could you say to them to make a difference?

SHOW LOVE

HEY—
ONE LAST THING...

Your community is not just you and your friends. It's designed for everyone who needs God in their lives. God wants to reach the hurting and the lonely, and He will equip you to help them and bring them to Him. Make sure you and your group are ready to help.

YOUR PRAYERS + THOUGHTS

Week 1	1	2	3	4	5	6	7
Week 2	8	9	10	11	12	13	14
Week 3	15	16	17	18	19	20	21
Week 4	22	23	24	25	26	27	28
Week 5	29	30	31	32	33	34	35
Week 6	36	37	38	39	**40**	41	42

BE READY FOR SOMEONE NEW!

DAY 41

If we want to grow in our faith, we have to learn what and whom we're going to allow to influence us. Then, we need to begin taking steps to consistently do the things that strengthen us.

For Tomorrow...

ON DAY 42, take the opportunity to go to church, attend your youth group, or pray and review this week's devotions.

PRESS PAUSE ⏸ **BETWEEN QUESTIONS** to reflect and write your answers.

Relax ⏸ PRESS

Situate yourself in a way that really lets you focus. Take a minute and ask God to help you soak up the truth of His word.

Read : 1 TIMOTHY 4:7–15

"Don't let anyone look down on you because you are young, but set an example for the believers in speech, in conduct, in love, in faith and in purity."

—*The Apostle Paul, writing to Timothy*

Relate : STEP INTO THIS PASSAGE OF SCRIPTURE

For a few moments, really try to get an understanding of the teaching and how it applies to your life.

1. Look at verse seven. What kind of myths and "wives tales" do you think might be influencing young people today? What untrue things is our culture telling us about ourselves, about God, and about others?

2. In verse eight we see that working out physically has some benefit, but where do we really see lasting benefit? Why do you think this is true?

3. Now, skip ahead to verse 16. What are some of the reasons why it is important to clearly know what you believe?

4. What impact does knowing what you believe have on others?

ReACT

5. Look at verses 11 through 13. What do these verses say young people should do in relation to other believers?

6. In what area(s) do you think you could be setting a better example? Do you need to set a better example in loving people? Ask God to show you where you need help.

7. Think about the schedule of your week. What percentage of your time do you spend on each of these activities:

Sleeping _____ Eating _____ TV _____ Internet _____
Phone _____ Job _____ Time alone with God _____
Time with friends _____ Church activities _____
Volunteering _____ Other _____

8. As you look over your answers, what do they say about your focus and what's important in your life? How would you like to see this change?

HEY—
ONE LAST THING...

SHOW LOVE

When you spend time with God, love others, and care for the hurting and suffering in the world, people will notice. I have met several people whose walk with God makes them seem really different. I say they "smell like Jesus," because the aroma of the Spirit of God emanates from them.

YOUR
PRAYERS +
THOUGHTS

Week 1	1	2	3	4	5	6	7
Week 2	8	9	10	11	12	13	14
Week 3	15	16	17	18	19	20	21
Week 4	22	23	24	25	26	27	28
Week 5	29	30	31	32	33	34	35
Week 6	36	37	38	39	40	**41**	42

DO YOU "SMELL LIKE JESUS"?

WATCH OUT FOR OPPORTUNITIES TO CHANGE A LIFE!

To Save A Life offers you a unique chance to use a movie and a powerful story as a conversation starter with your friends. It will set you up to talk about things that really matter—like your faith!

Talk to your coaches, youth workers or leaders about planning a *To Save A Life* movie event. Watch the movie with friends and then brainstorm about how you can reach out and help others on your campus. Some people are just dying to be heard. If you listen, you might discover a new friend and an opportunity to live an epic life together.

GET INVOLVED:

Find out how to make a difference at **ToSaveALifeMovie.com**.

SPEAKING OF SHARING— SHARING IS NICE!

• **IF YOU LIKED DEVO2GO™, TELL YOUR FRIENDS TO CHECK IT OUT—FOR FREE!** >> They can go to **Devo2Go.com** to download the first week. The download includes both the audio and the interactive journal.

• **ARTISTS: ON THE MOVIE WEBSITE IS A PLACE JUST FOR YOU** >> Share your artwork, and it just might be posted for the world to see!

• **TELL YOUR STORY** >> Post a message on the *Devo2Go*™ Facebook page to let us know how the movie and the devo impacted you, and how you're making a change on your campus. Send a picture and we might share your story with others.

> **"** Sharing **your** story can help others rewrite theirs! **"**
>
> —Leeland Mooring

MOVIE SITE:
ToSaveALifeMovie.com

FACEBOOK:
Facebook.com/ ToSaveALife

TWITTER:
Twitter.com/ ToSaveALife

FOR TEEN LEADERS & ADULTS:
ToSaveALifeLeaders.com

DEVO2GO:
Devo2Go.com

SPREAD THE LOVE!

Life is a journey, and it's better to travel it with others. Below are a few things you can do right where you are:

myspace + facebook + twitter + email

• **USE YOUR MYSPACE, FACEBOOK, TWITTER OR OTHER SOCIAL NETWORKS TO DO GOOD** >> Join the *ToSaveALife* groups on these sites, follow us and learn what others are doing to make a difference. You can find links on the movie website.

• **EACH DAY, POST A NOTE OF ENCOURAGEMENT** >> Tell someone you care or leave a friend a message to brighten their day. Invest yourself in others and see how the ripples of your life can make an impact.

• **START A GROUP** >> On campus or online, bring people together from different backgrounds and different communities.

 Don't forget! Go back over your journal notes in *Devo2Go*™ and look for the places where you made comments about things you wanted to do—or do differently. Highlight them so you don't forget, and then begin to live them out!

> "When you live out the mission God created you to do, it's then that He whispers in response, **"My masterpiece!"**

—Jim Britts

GRAB YOUR GEAR!

On **ToSaveALifeMovie.com**, you'll find a link for official *To Save A Life* gear, like t-shirts, books, slap bracelets, and encouragement stickers for your friends.

• **STICKERS** >> Use these to reach out and lift up your friends!

• **SLAP BRACELETS + T-SHIRTS** >> not only look cool, they're great for starting conversations!

And, see the last few pages in this journal for more information on *To Save A Life* books.

plus...
FREE STUFF!

Make sure you sign up on **ToSaveALifeMovie.com** to receive announcements about free stuff like music and other cool items...and don't forget to send the first week of *Devo2Go*™ to a friend for FREE!

CURRICULUM KIT

Everything a youth leader needs to plan
and implement a seven-week series >>

Tell Your
**YOUTH
LEADER!**

- Includes movie clips from
  To Save A Life for each session

- Features a wealth of support
  materials, including Leader's
  Guide, sermons, activities,
  movie-branded graphics
  + invitational tools

- Helps teens fall in love with
  God and begin acting out
  their faith as Jesus would—
  by reaching out to the lost,
  left out, hurting, and lonely
  on their school campuses

- Written and tested by a
  seasoned youth pastor

Look for *To Save A Life* Curriculum Kit at your local Christian
bookstore, or visit **Outreach.com** for bulk quantities.